miles d

MW00862392

Arranged by Brent Edstrom and James Sodke

contents

2   All Blues

6   Blue in Green

8   Boplicity (Be Bop Lives)

18   Circle

13   Dig

26   Eighty One

34   Flamenco Sketches

31   Four

38   Freddie Freeloader

41   Half Nelson

44   Miles

49   Milestones

54   Nardis

58   Seven Steps to Heaven

61   So What

64   Solar

69   Somethin' Else

76   The Theme

74   Tune Up

Front cover photo by Rault Jean Francois/CORBIS KIPA

ISBN 978-0-634-05905-6

HAL•LEONARD®
CORPORATION
7777 W. BLUEMOUND RD. P.O. BOX 13819 MILWAUKEE, WI 53213

Visit Hal Leonard Online at
www.halleonard.com

ALL BLUES

By MILES DAVIS

BLUE IN GREEN

By MILES DAVIS

BOPLICITY
(Be Bop Lives)

By MILES DAVIS
and GIL EVANS

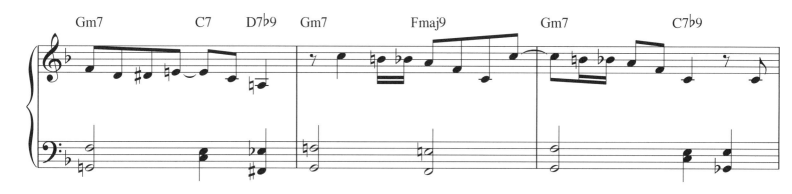

D.S. al Coda
(with repeat)

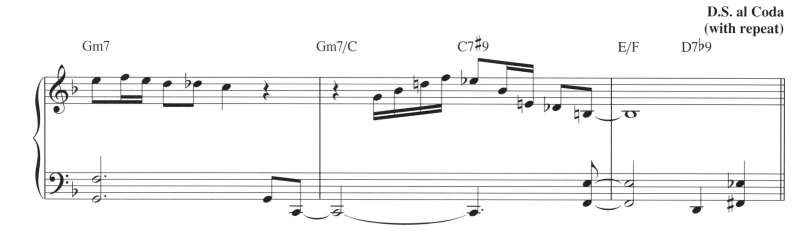

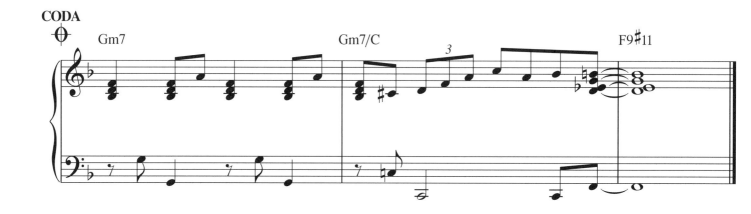

DIG

By MILES DAVIS

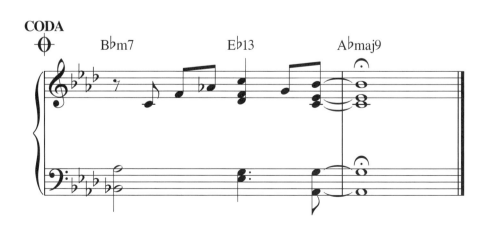

CIRCLE

By MILES DAVIS

EIGHTY ONE

By MILES DAVIS
and RONALD CARTER

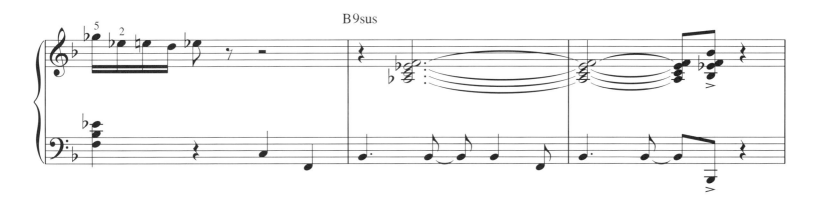

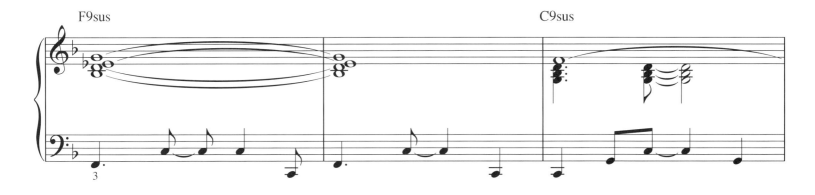

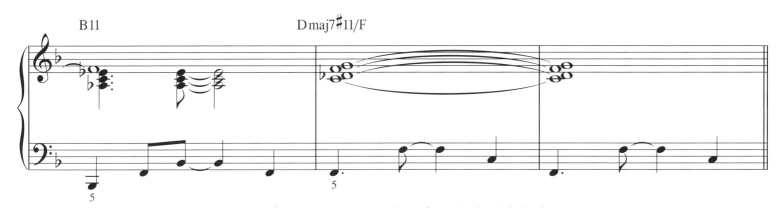

FOUR

By MILES DAVIS

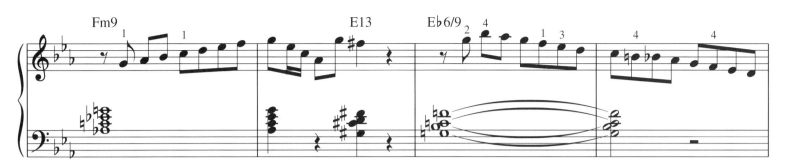

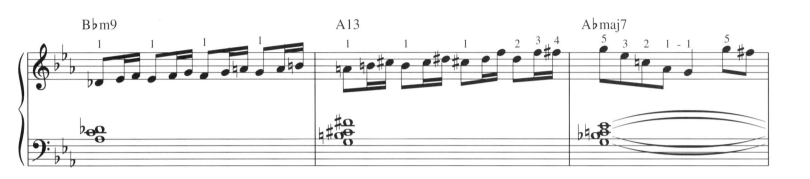

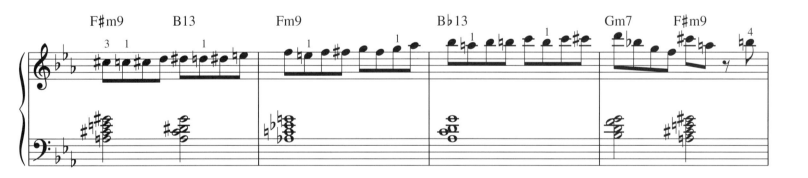

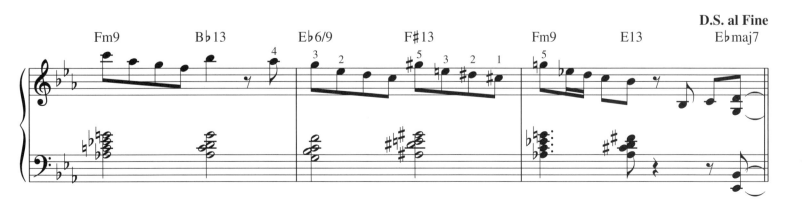

FLAMENCO SKETCHES

By MILES DAVIS

Slow Ballad

FREDDIE FREELOADER

By MILES DAVIS

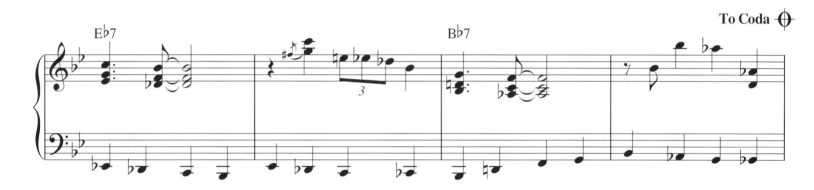

HALF NELSON

By MILES DAVIS

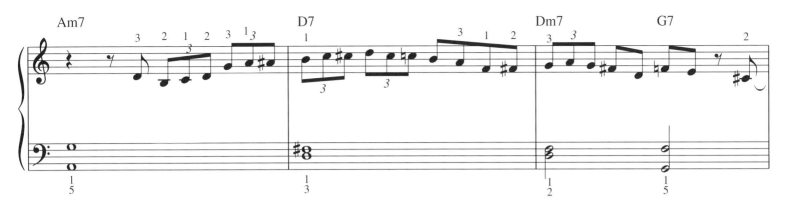

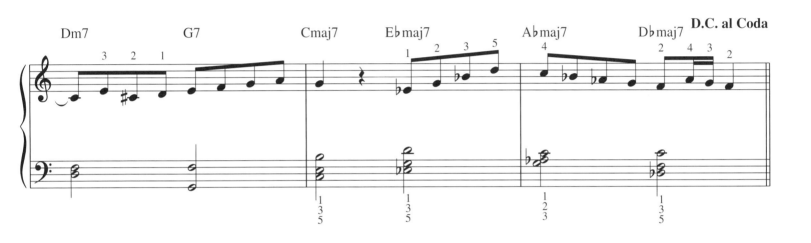

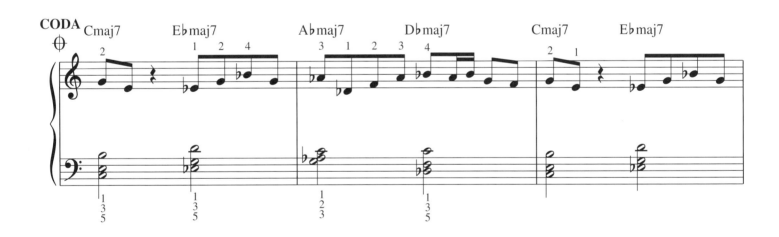

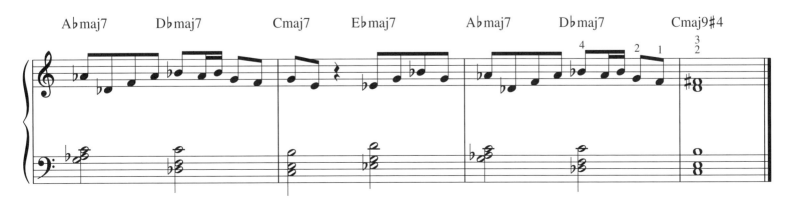

MILES

By MILES DAVIS

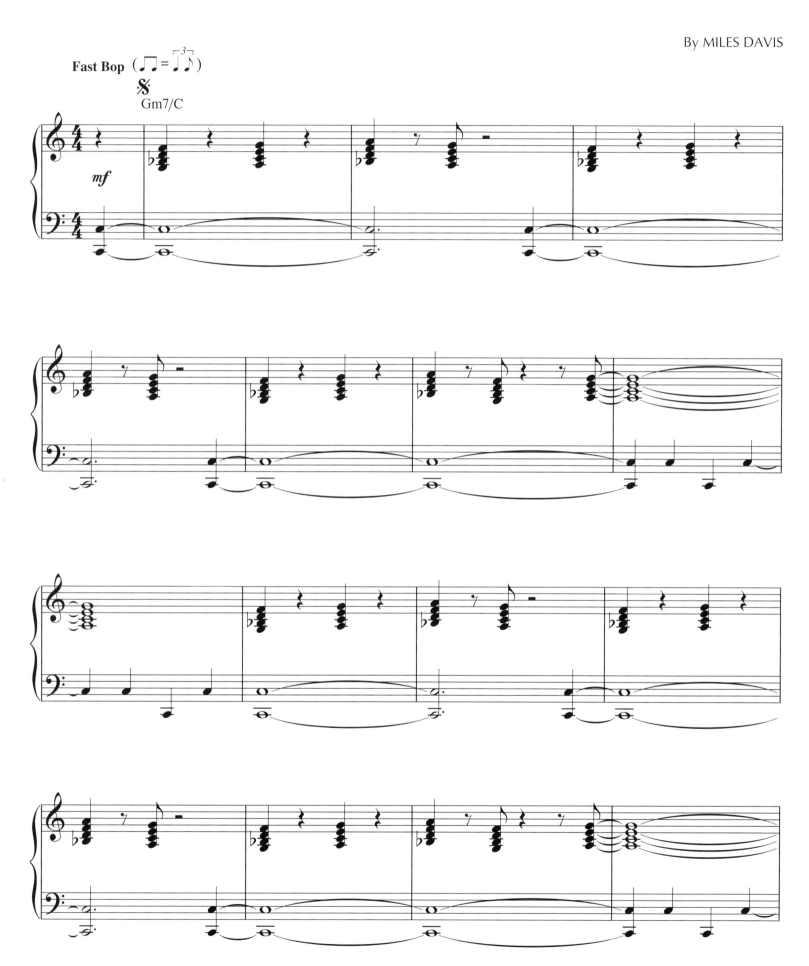

Am7

MILESTONES

By MILES DAVIS

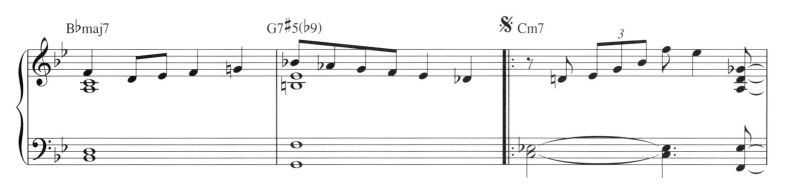

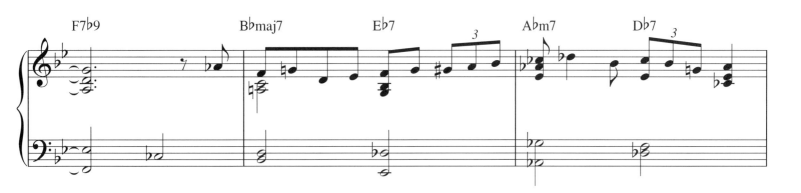

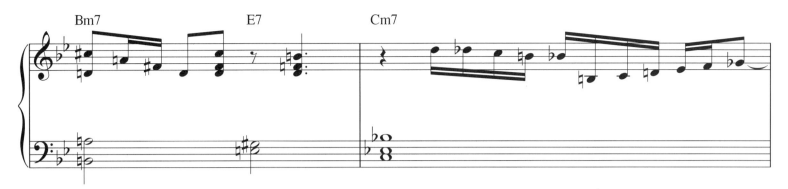

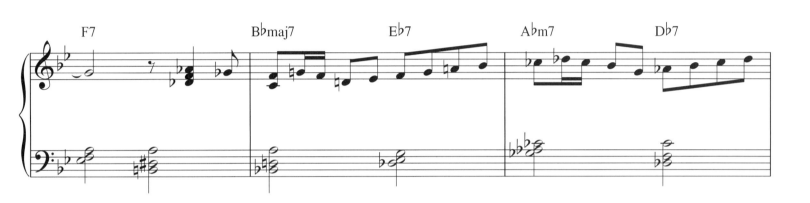

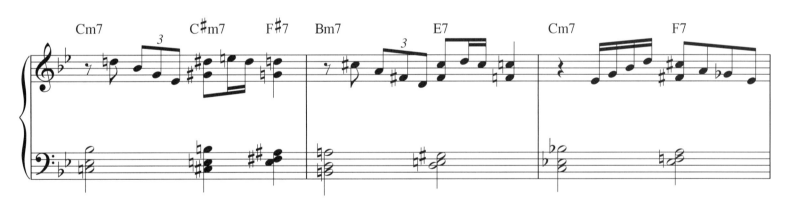

D.S. al Coda

CODA

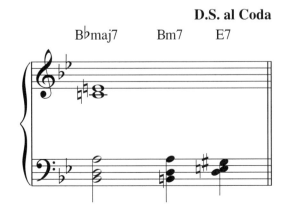

NARDIS

By MILES DAVIS

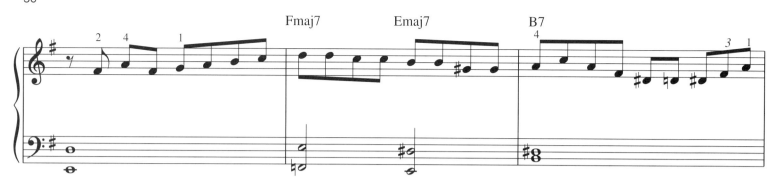

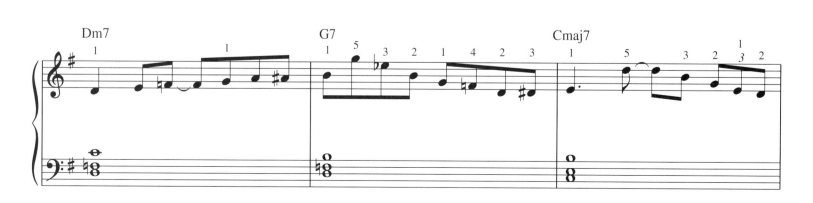

SEVEN STEPS TO HEAVEN

By MILES DAVIS
and VICTOR FELDMAN

60

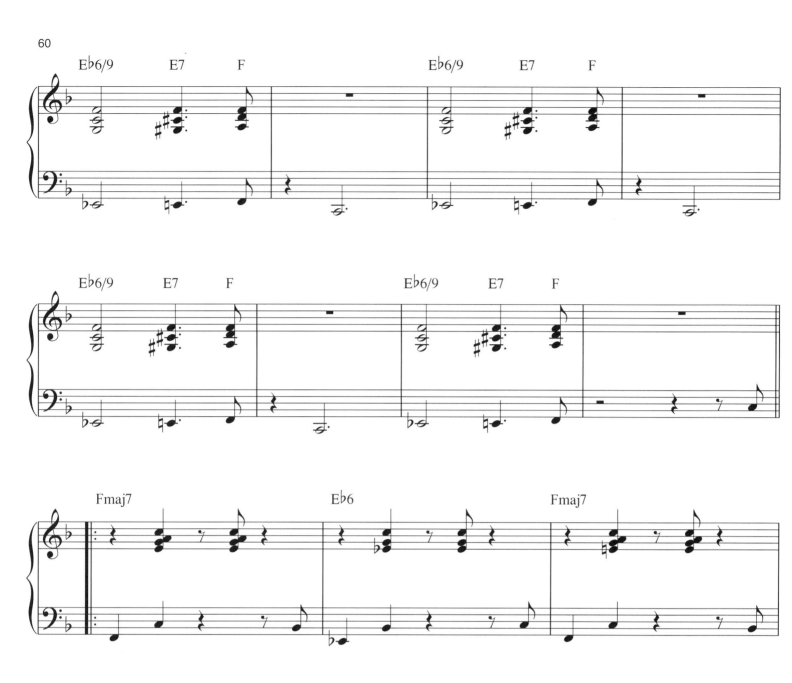

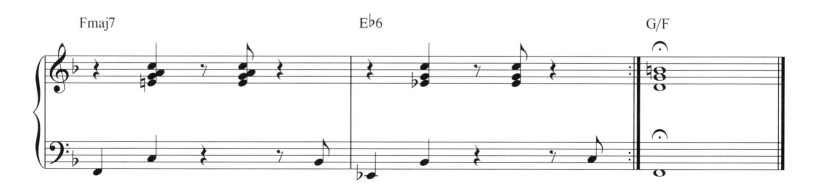

SO WHAT

By MILES DAVIS

SOLAR

By MILES DAVIS

Medium Swing

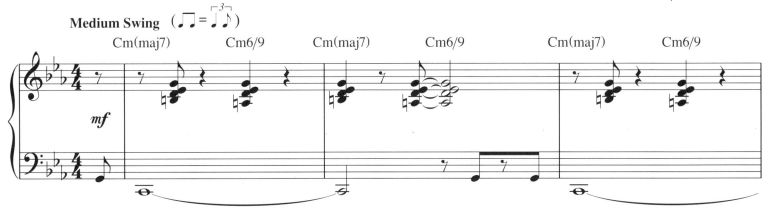

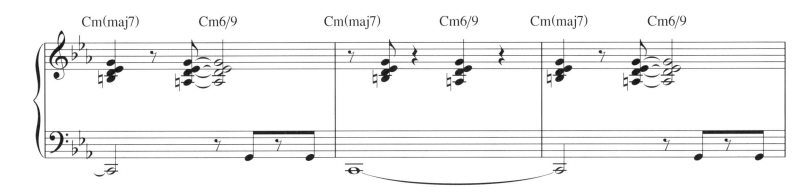

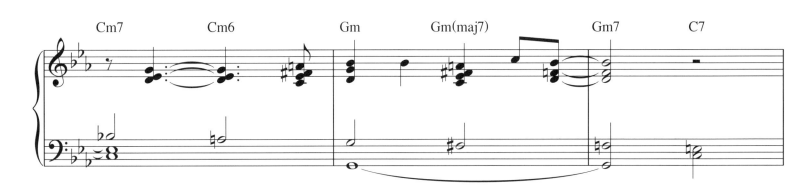

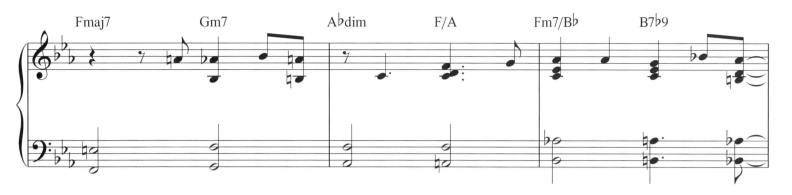

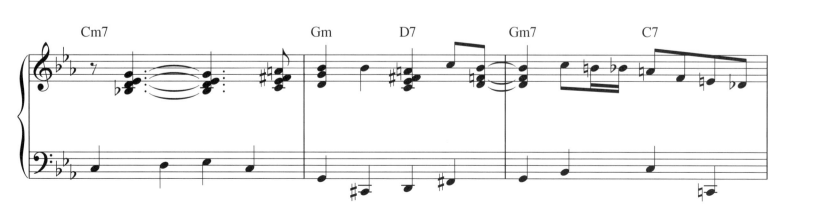

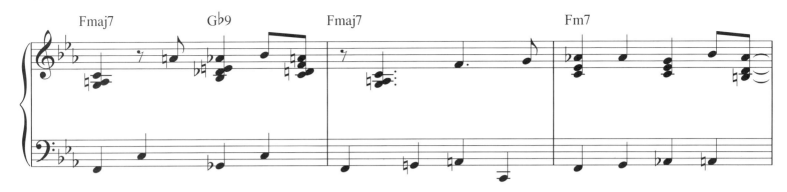

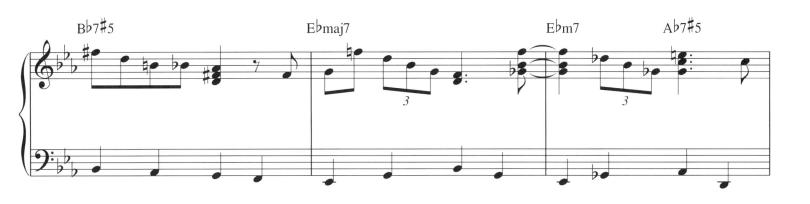

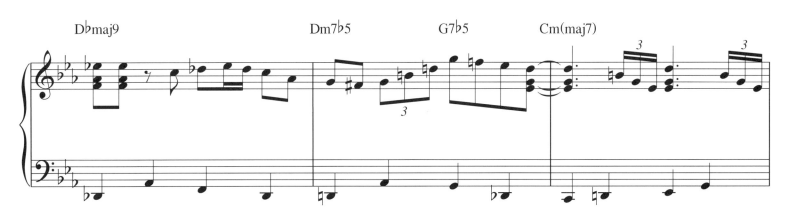

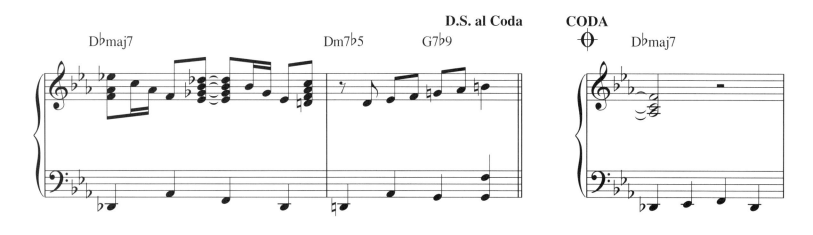

SOMETHIN' ELSE

By MILES DAVIS

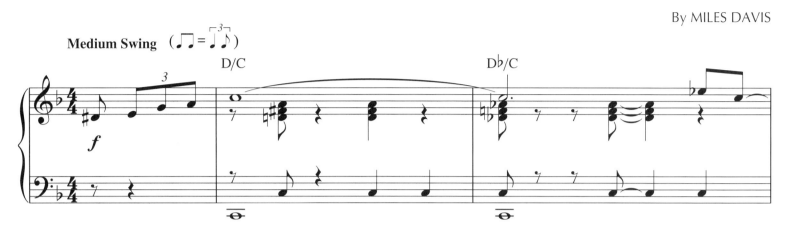

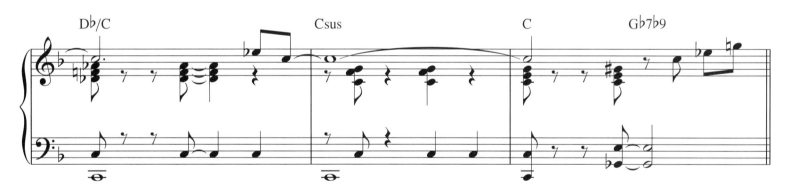

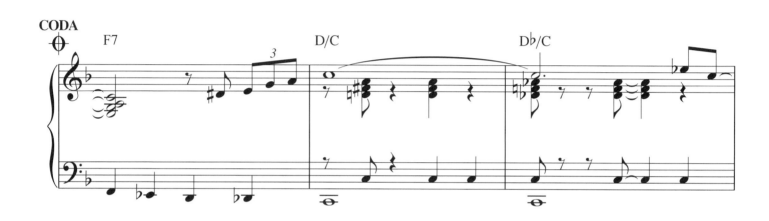

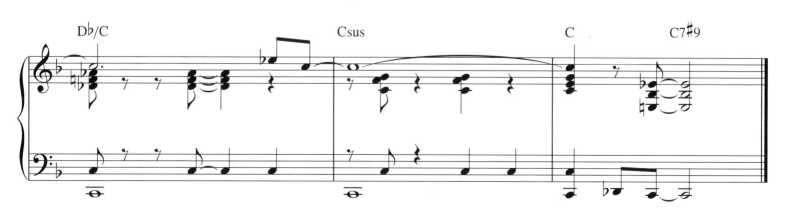

TUNE UP

By MILES DAVIS

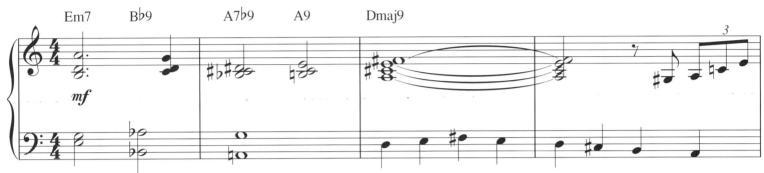

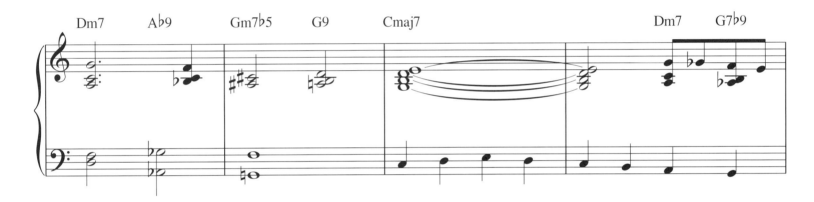

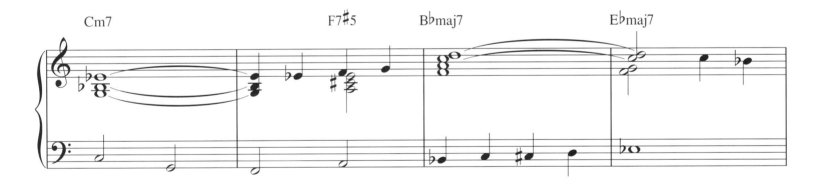

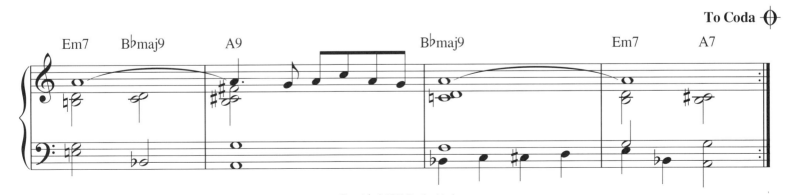

THE THEME

By MILES DAVIS

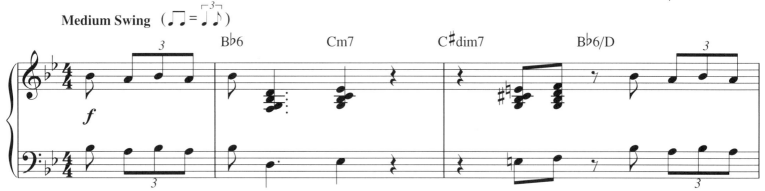

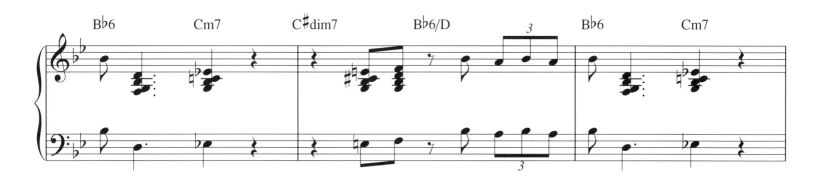

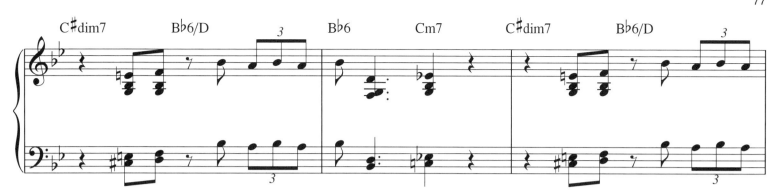

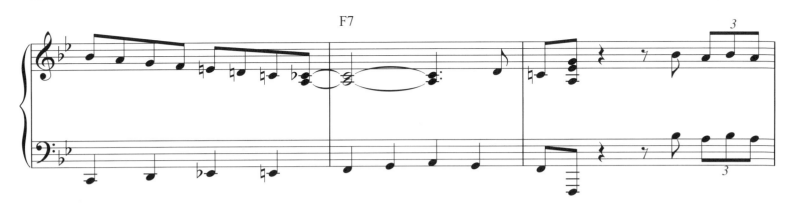